NORTH YORK MOORS

THROUGH TIME

Paul Chrystal &
Mark Sunderland

AMBERLEY PUBLISHING

Acknowledgements

Thanks go to James Lake, Rocastle Books for many of the pictures of Guisborough; to Paul Gaythorpe, www.pk4images.com for the colour image on p.18; to Lesley Skipper for permission to use the black and white pictures of Swainby and Whorlton on pages 57 and 59 taken from her book *The Castle on the Hill;* to Chris Pearson of the Laurence Stern Trust for permission to reproduce the card on p.96, to Selfmadehero publishers for permission to reproduce the page from Martin Rowson's version of *Tristram Shandy;* to Anne Cartwright, Robert Thompson's Craftsmen Ltd, for permission to use the vintage Robert Thompson pictures on pages 73, 75 and 76; to Cllr Frances Greenwell for permission to photograph the Captain Cook Schoolroom Museum; Helmsley Archaeological and Historical Society for the illustration on page 81; and to Les Almond who spotted things to which I was blind or oblivious, or both.

for Les

More of Mark Sunderland's work can be found at www.marksunderland.com
For more books on Yorkshire go to www.knaresboroughbookshop.com

First published 2010

Amberley Publishing
Cirencester Road, Chalford,
Stroud, Gloucestershire, GL6 8PE

www.amberley-books.com

Copyright © Paul Chrystal & Mark Sunderland, 2010

The right of Paul Chrystal & Mark Sunderland to be identified as the Authors of this work has been asserted in accordance with the Copyrights, Designs and Patents Act 1988.

ISBN 978 1 84868 898 8

British Library Cataloguing in Publication Data.
A catalogue record for this book is available from the British Library.

Typeset in 9.5pt on 12pt Celeste.
Typesetting by Amberley Publishing.
Printed in the UK.

Introduction

The North York Moors is one of Britain's most beautiful and picturesque rural areas, much of which is enclosed in the North York Moors National Park. This book provides an at-a-glance picture of that beauty through 200 or so images which show particular parts of the Moors at the end of the nineteenth and the early twentieth century and how those same places look today in 2010. Some have changed a lot, others not so much and others have changed completely or have gone for good. The black and white and corresponding contemporary colour pictures are complemented by informative captions which explain the photographs and in so doing provide a brief history of the towns, villages, people, industries and social activities depicted. The book is wide ranging: it covers the Moors from Guisborough in the north to Coxwold and Helmsley in the south, from Osmotherley in the west to Fylingdales in the east.

The National Park itself covers 553 square miles, 40% of which is open moorland and is the largest expanse of heather in England producing an estimated 3 million flowers per square mile. It rises to almost 1450 feet. Fifty thousand sheep graze here. But it wasn't always quite as serene. Travelling through the Moors today it is hard, almost impossible, to remember that large areas were given over to mining. Alum and ironstone were mined extensively around Guisborough, Swainby, Goathland, Rosedale and Beck Hole; evidence of this industrial heritage can still be seen but it is sporadic and the natural beauty of each of these places has long reclaimed them. Nothing is demonstrated more clearly by the *Through Time* concept of then and now that underpins this book.

The social and economic effects of the railways are also covered as is the influence of affluent, sometimes philanthropic, landowners like the Chaloners in Guisborough and Sir Charles Duncombe and later Earls of Feversham in Helmsley.

Religion too played a big role in the area. Apart from abbeys and priories like Mount Grace, Byland, Rievaulx and Guisborough, Quakers, Methodists and the good works of ebullient and charismatic men of the cloth like Canon John Latimer Kyle at Carlton, the Revd Lawrence Sterne in Coxwold and the Revd Charles Norris Gray in Helmsely all enliven the book. Indeed, the area can boast a large number of characters important in various, more secular, walks of life: in literature there is Sterne of course, the founder of modern comic writing with *Tristram Shandy*, and cameo appearances by William and Dorothy Wordsworth and Dickens; John Christopher Atkinson, ornithologist and author of the celebrated *Forty Years in a Moorland Parish;* Robert "Mouseman" Thompson and his world famous furniture workshop at Kilburn; Catherine Parr and Oliver Cromwell; John Oxlee, linguist extraordinaire; the giant Henry Cooper, the Maharajah of the Punjab and the eccentric Sultan of Zanzibar. All of these are celebrated here along with genuine icons like Lilla Cross, the White Horse at Kilburn and Fylingdales Ballistic Early Warning Station which between them span fourteen centuries of Moors life.

The North York Moors are famous for the mystery and intrigue they have generated over the years. The Hand of Glory in Castleton, bottomless Lake Gormire, The Hole of Horcum, the wizard-like John Wrightson and HMS *Prima Prilius* cruising down Stokesley High Street – all resonate with their own mystery and magic.

Mark Sunderland, professional landscape photographer, has taken all the new, colour photographs. The scenery of the Moors has allowed him to exploit his expertise to recreate the unique moods and ambience of the towns, villages and landscapes featured in this book in a truly original and exciting way.

A book like this is wholly dependent on the early photographs and postcards that are available at the time of writing; for that reason the book is far from exhaustive and many places could not be included. It is hoped that a second volume will follow soon, so if you have pictures that we can use then please do contact me. The places on and around the Moors that are included are: Guisborough, Upleatham, Slape Wath, Claphow, Mulgrave Castle, Great Ayton, Stokesley, Danby, Castleton, Lealholm, Glaisdale, Egton Bridge, Grosmont, Goathland, Beck Hole, Carlton, Swainby, Whorlton, Potto, Osmotherley, Chop Gate, Hole of Horcum, Fylingdales, Rosedale Abbey, Hawnby, Hutton-le-Hole, Sutton Bank, Kilburn, Helmsley and Coxwold.

Paul Chrystal 2010
p@chrystal30.fsnet.co.uk

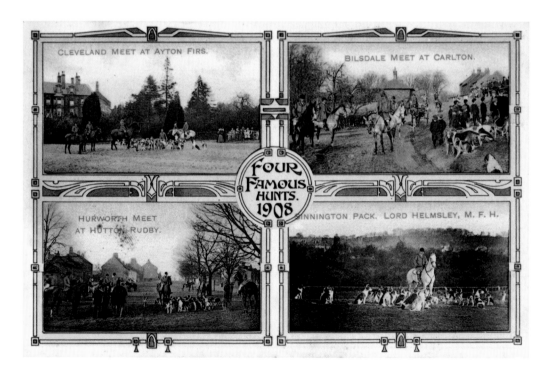

Four Famous Hunts

NORTH YORK MOORS

THROUGH TIME

Guisborough Market Place 1891

In the nineteenth century the corn and butter markets were held on Tuesdays with the general market on each Saturday. The wool market took place on 27 June and 25 July while the servants hiring fairs were on the last Tuesday in April and the second Tuesday in November. The cross is from the 1800s, the gas lamps somewhat later. Note the sundial and ball finial on the top. The 1876 public urinal can be seen in the background beyond the cross. It was eventually removed in 1892 after much public protest and an alternative was built in Bakehouse Square. The building on the left is the Town Hall bearing the arms of the Chaloners on the gable. The ground floor and first storey were built in 1821 with a second storey added in 1850 in a different style. The arches were originally open and housed a shambles, or meat market. Traffic apart the scene is still familiar today.

Browns *Nil Simile* Footware

Number 32 Market Place, officially recorded as cordwainers, the old name for shoe and boot suppliers. Browns – a cobblers with a difference – moved to number 22 some years later. The Golden Lion is to the left. Over the years Guisborough has been variously called Ghigesburg, Gisbourne and Gisbrough. Gisborough is still retained in references to the Priory, Lord Gisborough and the Gisborough estate. From about 1550 the Chaloner family became synonymous with Guisborough: Admiral Thomas Chaloner of Long Hull (1815-1884) in particular, started off a long tradition of philanthropy and involvement in local affairs.

Post Office – Open all Hours!
In Westgate in the late nineteenth century, moving to Chaloner Street in 1902. It was open on weekdays from 7.00am to 8.00pm with seven despatches and three deliveries at 7.45am, 1.00pm and 5.10pm. On Sundays it opened 8.00am to 10.00am with a delivery at 9.30am. The building here was then occupied by a chemist's, as it is still today. Note the children with their hula-hoops; the man in the new picture looks lost without his. Robert de Brus, one of William the Conqueror's most dependable supporters, received land from him establishing his seat at Skelton Castle, five miles to the east of Guisborough. In 1119 Robert de Brus II founded the Augustinian Priory here with the backing of Pope Calixtus II and Archbishop Thurston of York.

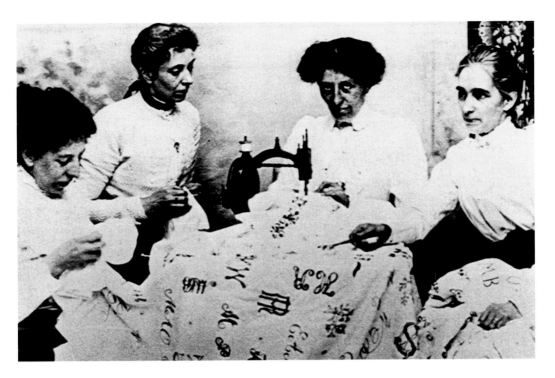

The Guisborough Quilt and the Fat Eighth

A fundraising event in 1904 as part of the town bazaar to raise money for the restoration of St Nicholas' Parish Church. Anyone wanting to contribute had to pay for a square which was then embroidered with their initials. It was obviously a success as Temple Moore, the architect, took on the project from 1904-1907. Old traditions die hard as the modern picture shows.

General Booth comes to Guisborough

General Booth, founder of the Salvation Army, visited Guisborough on a number of occasions. This visit in 1905 gave an opportunity for an early motorcade along Westgate. "Get Saved" the banners exclaim. Fairs were held in Westgate twice a year but these soon outgrew the space and moved to Fair Fields, now a housing development. Guisborough's population in the late 1600s was about 1,000, mostly engaged in farming. By 1801 it had risen to 1,719 and by 1870 over 1,600 Guisborough men were engaged in mining.

The Guisborough Co-op and *Très Bon Beer*

The Co-op reached Guisborough in 1873 moving to a converted house in Westgate in 1905 as shown here; the original name was the Industrial and Provident Society. It paid a dividend of 2s in the £ in 1885 – bettered by the somewhat concerned local competition with a 2s 6d dividend. The butchery department was next to the Three Fiddlers Inn whose sign read: *"Extremely Free House… Très Bon Beer"* in fluent franglais. The elegant upstairs windows and coving have survived.

Church Street 1920s

Taken in the 1920s, the buildings on the right have all been demolished which now affords a view of the Priory. The window and door of the Abbey Café were removed to the Castle Museum in York as one of their street exhibitions. St Nicholas' Parish church is at the end of the street presumably on the site of the original church mentioned in *Domesday*. On the left are the Priory Ice-cream Saloon, George Wear's at 13-15, baker and confectioner, café and Temperance Hotel: *"Pic-nic Parties and Schools catered for, Refreshments at moderate charges. Agents for Lipton's Teas."*

The Red Lion, Church Street

Taken in the early twentieth century this shows proprietor James Fawns with serving and canine security staff. Fawns' name can still be seen above the doorway leading to where the pub yard used to be. The building is now occupied by a hairdresser's. John Oxlee was born in Guisborough in 1779 – one of the world's greatest linguists, proficient in an astonishing 123 different languages and dialects; he often had to compile his own grammars and dictionaries, so rare were some of them. One of his most celebrated books was *One Hundred and More Vocabularies as from the Stamina of Human Speed Commencing with the Hungarian and Terminating with Yoruba,* published in 1840. You won't find that on Amazon.

The Fox Inn, Bow Street

In Bow Street in the early days of motoring, Mr and Mrs Sutcliffe stand proudly outside with the garage man and more canine security. In the early 1820s the pub was run by a Mr Knaggs and it was the coaching inn for the run to Whitby. You can still see the original mounting steps outside the front door. The pub was rebuilt in 1926 when the Newcastle Brewery bought it and introduced letting bedrooms on the first floor.

The Empire Picture House and Cherry Kearton's Travelling Menagerie

The opening of the Empire Picture Hall in Chaloner Street in 1911 much to the delight of hundreds of Guisborough children. Cherry Kearton was top of the bill – the famous Yorkshire naturalist, wildlife photographer and film maker who travelled the world much like a latter day David Attenborough. One of his more famous assignments was with Teddy (twenty-sixth president of the USA) and Kermit (his son) Roosevelt visiting British East Africa (Kenya) in 1909 for a safari. They travelled on the *Lunatic Express* from Mombasa later releasing the footage as a silent film entitled *Roosevelt in Africa*. 250 local guides and porters were hired to set up huge tent cities and carry the equipment and tons of salt for skin preservation. Roosevelt's tent had a bath and a library of 60 books. The expedition collected 23,151 natural history specimens: 160 species of carnivores, ungulates, rodents, insectivores, and bats. Mammals alone accounted for 5,013 specimens, including nine lions, thirteen rhinoceros, twenty zebras, eight warthogs, and four hyenas. It took eight years to catalogue all of the material. The cinema was converted from the old tannery as the signs on the left indicate.

Queen Victoria's Diamond Jubilee 1897

All over Britain villages, towns and cities were decked out to celebrate Victoria's fifty years on the throne as Queen and Empress. Guisborough of course was no exception as the specially created archway at the junction of Bow Street, Church Street and Market Place shows. The cross is done up like a Christmas Tree decorated with evergreen foliage and lanterns. At the time Britain ruled nearly a quarter of the world's land mass (11 million square miles) and a quarter of the world's inhabitants; the parade of people from all parts of the Empire in London took 45 minutes to pass by. A similar celebration took place here for Edward VII's coronation in 1902.

Northgate Demolition 1950

This shows workmen in October 1959 beginning the demolition of Northgate cottages, later to be replaced by flats – part of the ongoing programme in the '50s and '60s to provide sanitary and clean housing for all. The water supply in Bank Street was condemned by the Medical Officer in the early twentieth century because the service pipe had been laid under middens.

Guisborough Cricket Club

The earliest evidence for cricket in Guisborough goes as far back as 1820; matches were banned on Sundays, and it is recorded that the *"Parish Constable was paid nine shillings for assisting in detecting players who played on Sundays."* The club joined the North Yorkshire Cricket league in 1895 two years after its inauguration and promptly won the championship in its first season. Membership cost 7s 6d. Fixtures included Redcar, Ironopolis (Middlesbrough), West Hartlepool and Constable Burton. Colours were maroon and gold. The club built a new pavilion at Fountains Garth in 1912 at a cost of £350 – the money raised by a Grand Bazaar in the Priory Grounds. More recently there have been four successive wins in 2001 to 2004 making Guisborough the first club to win four successive championships on two occasions. The modern photograph shows a recent match against Northerallerton: batsman is Ian Gill (top scorer for Northallerton with 101); Guisborough wicket keeper is Gary Veazey.

Guisborough Priory, The Wine Cellar.

Gisborough Priory Wine Cellar

The thirteenth-century vaulted cellarium has nine bays. The Norman gatehouse at the western end is all that survives of the original Priory and only because in the sixteenth and seventeenth centuries it was used as an entrance to the Chaloner mansion in Bow Street. The cloisters and the nave of the church were removed and formal gardens were established by 1709. The cloister had become a sunken bowling green by this time.

Gisborough Priory and the Careless Plumber

Founded in 1119 Robert de Brus' Augustinian Priory of St Mary of Gyseburn was rebuilt in the thirteenth and fourteenth centuries after a devastating fire in 1289 caused by a careless plumber who was mending the roof and left some charcoal burning when he left off for a break. The Priory assumed local rights for trading, manufacturing and sand mining and it was this that dictated the economic and social development of Guisborough and the surrounding area for centuries to come. Annual income of the Priory in 1535 was £628 6s 8d – the fourth largest in Yorkshire. After the Dissolution it passed to the Chaloner family in 1550 who became lords of the manor. The surviving eastern gable is 97 feet high. The bucolic picture of the priory is from the cover of Gordon Home's *Yorkshire Coast and Moorland*, A&C Black 1915.

Ambulance Crash on Upleatham Bridge

An unfortunate incident where a British Red Cross – St John's Ambulance crashed through the parapet of Upleatham Bridge. Admiral Thomas Chaloner had established the Miner's Accident Hospital in 1873 (it later became a cottage hospital); in 1886 it admitted forty-nine patients including thirteen miners. An X-ray department, outpatients' clinic and operating theatre opened in 1928; the hospital closed in 1982. In 1888 the town's death rate was 18 per 100, mostly children under the age of five – 28% were children under a year old – 51% of these died from bronchitis or pneumonia. This was popularly attributed to parents "hardening up" their children by taking them out in the evening or to church services. A less dramatic picture is conveyed by the new photograph.

Upleatham Church Nr. Guisborough   16975

Upleatham Church – Britain's Smallest Church?

Upleatham claims to be one of the smallest churches in Britain at eighteen feet by fifteen. It boasts a Norman nave although the tower is seventeenth century. The last service here was held in 1836; the church was fully restored in October 1966 by men from B Company, 4th Battalion The Green Howards based in Middlesbrough. The alum mines nearby are thought to owe their origin to Sir Thomas Chaloner who, after a visit to the Pope's mines at Puteoli, brought back the secret details of efficient alum extraction techniques along with a number of specialist artisans who had been concealed in wooden cases; the Vatican controlled most to the world's supply of alum at the time. For this early act of industrial espionage and people trafficking Sir Thomas was excommunicated. Before Chaloner Britain was paying the Papal States £52 per ton; Chaloner was able to charge £11 per ton. Alum was used in the dying of wool – and wool at the time was Britain's biggest industry – as well as other textiles, tanning and candlemaking.

Slapewath Ironstone Mine

The Slapewath (*slippery crossing* in Old English) Mine was started by Thomas Charlton in 1864 close to the village named after him. The shafts date from 1880 when the mine was being operated by Samuelson & Co. The downcast shaft now surrounded by a high wall is 286 feet deep. Apart from the mine Slapewath is famous for its mineral springs, discovered in 1822 by the Revd James Wilcock, Head of the Grammar School. The spa enjoyed some popularity until the mid 1800s. The fine housing remains but the mine building and the tower are long gone.

Claphow Double Rail Bridge

On Stanghow Road this unusual construction owes its peculiar appearance to mining subsidence: the bridge being reinforced with a second arch inside the original. A buttress was added on the right hand side and four iron rods inserted through the parapet; the left hand side was concreted. The railways largely took over from boats in the transportation of alum. This included the importation of large quantities of urine from Hull and London to supplement what was left out on doorsteps locally. Urine was added to produce ammonium which was then added to liquid alum and boiled to produce alum crystals.

Mulgrave Castle and the Maharajah of the Punjab

The original Norman castle was a royalist garrison slighted in 1647. The later castle, a castellated mansion, was built for the Duchess of Buckingham (Lady Catherine Darnley), James II's illegitimate daughter who married the Earl of Mulgrave. The surrounding woodlands were landscaped by William Repton in 1792 and feature an amazing artificial battery called the Quarter Deck (see inset) which was danced on by Charles Dickens in 1844. In 1858 Dalip Singh Sukerchakia, the last Maharajah of the Punjab, stayed here with his elephants for five years; in 1860 he paid for two miles of road to be built leading to the mansion because his elephants were irritated by sand between their toes. Initially it was a toll road: 1d for a horse; ½d for a pig; 9d for a 3-wheeled motorcar; 1/- for a 4-wheeled car. The property is owned by Constantine Phipps, 5th Marquess of Normanby.

Mulgrave Castle, from the Quarter Deck.

Great Ayton Leven Side

The Royal Oak is in the middle here and still serves today; horse and cart ouside Cockerills the butcher's and handcart outside the Middlesbrough Cooperative Society drapery and grocer's with a Cadbury's cocoa advert in the window. Ayton means river farm; *Domesday* has it as *Aytun*. In the 1800s the population was 600, one third of whom were engaged in the local linen industry. Newton Road off the High Street is known locally as California after the influx of mineworkers in the nineteenth century – about 800 Ayton men are thought to have been employed in the ironstone mines. Great Ayton was never famous for its wild social life – due to the lack of a market and the influence of the Quakers: in 1890 there were only two inns while in nearby Stokesley which was smaller at the time there were fourteen. In 1896 a Ladies Dance Quartette was permitted to go ahead only because there was *'no exposure of the limbs, as, if held up at an angle of 90 degrees [the dress] is so fully pleated that it does not even expose the underskirt at all'.*

The Friends' School, Great Ayton

George Fox, founder of the Society of Friends probably visited Great Ayton and Guisborough on his tour of the North York Moors around 1650 after he had heard that *"the seed was in Cleveland."* The Quakers established a Meeting House at High Green in 1700. Thomas Richardson, a retired banker known as "The Friend in Lombard Street"' and investor with George Stephenson in the Stockton and Darlington Railway and in the Middlesbrough Estate which resulted in the development of that town, founded the Friends' School in 1841 along with a 70 acre estate as an agricultural boarding school for 36 boys and 36 girls: the North of England Agricultural School for Girls & Boys. The curriculum included Latin, Euclid, physiology and agriculture – for the boys; girls were trained in domestic work. The mission statement was similarly pragmatic and unenterprising: *"to fit young people of both sexes to be useful and happy in those circles in which an unerring Creator has placed them, rather than prompt them to aspire after the more elevated walks of life".* In effect this meant farm labouring. Pupil numbers quickly rose to over 200. In 1991 the school changed its name to the more secular Ayton School but was forced to close in 1997: over the 157 years of its existence nearly 7,500 pupils and 550 teachers passed through its doors. The estate was bought by Wimpey who have developed it for private housing.

Captain James Cook RN, FRS

Great Ayton is Captain James Cook's village; he moved there with his family from Marton to Aireyholme Farm in 1736. Their later stone cottage was meticulously taken down brick by brick and transported to Point Hicks near Melbourne – the place in Australia Cook first set eyes on – to be rebuilt. Even the sloping of the walls was copied and creepers growing round the cottage were dug up, transported and transplanted. An obelisk marks the spot now, built from stone from Point Hicks – poor recompense. The statue on High Green has Cook age sixteen looking towards Staithes where he first felt the lure of the sea. The sculpture was commissioned by Hambleton District Council and is by sculptor Nicholas Dimbleby. It was unveiled on 12 May 1997.

AYTON SCHOOL.—COOKERY SCHOOL.

Great Ayton Schools

The older picture shows a girls' cookery class in full swing at the Friends' School while the newer one depicts a scene from Cook's classroom reconstructed in the Captain Cook Schoolroom Museum. It is housed in what was a charity school which was founded in 1704 by Michael Postgate, a local landowner. Here, between 1736 and 1740, Cook received his early, and only formal, education.

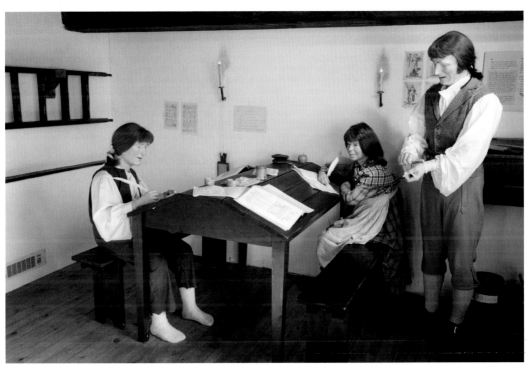

Great Ayton, Old Church. 942

All Saints Church

The old All Saints Church, made redundant in 1876, which has fragments of eighth-century Saxon crosses, a Norman doorway, nave, font and chancel, is particularly relevant to the Cook family. Thomas Skottowe is buried there – the man who spotted Cook's potential and paid for his education and then his apprenticeship at William Sanderson's grocer's in Staithes. The 1743 sundial over the porch is still working and bears the inscription: *horas non numero nisi serenas.* Five of James' brothers and sisters four of whom died before age five are also buried there along with Grace, his mother. Cook's 51 feet high monument is 1,000 feet above the village on Easby Moor; erected in 1827 it reads: *"massacred at Owyhee".* The spot where he died on Hawaii was bought for Britain and has since been maintained by the Royal Navy.

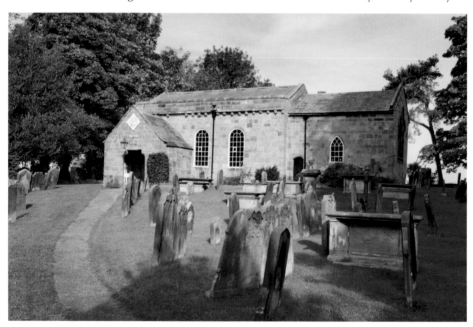

Stokesley Town Hall

Built in 1853 in the Italian style by Colonel R. Hildyard to replace an earlier town hall and "ancient and unsightly" toll booth where court sessions and market business was conducted. It also housed a Reading Room, Mechanics Institution library and the Langbaurgh West Savings' Bank (£30,023 deposited there by 911 depositors in 1856). A market cross, destroyed in 1783 when a bonfire built to celebrate a naval victory got out of hand, stood in the small square behind. This was originally The Shambles, or butcher's market which comprised twenty-four butchers' shops; nearby was a fish market and a police station and lock-up where the police station now stands. The area in front of the town hall is known as The Plain; there was a butter market near here at one time. Called Stocheslage in the eleventh century, Stokesley comes from stoke (wood) and ley (meadow). William Rufus gave the village and surrounding lands to Guy de Baliol.

Levenside and HMS _Primus Prilius_ Sailing down the High Street

Stokesley has been plagued by floods over many years, notably in 1929 and 1976. In 1939 the Ministry of Defence commissioned Burness Ship Building Company to provide flat-bottomed tugboats for use in transferring troops across shallow waters. Flooding at Stokesley provided just the right conditions and so the town was chosen as the test centre in 1939. Residents were astonished to see the HMS _Prima Prilius_ cruising up and down the High Street one morning for over an hour; the cameras of enterprising photographers were confiscated.

College Square

The Preston Grammar School was in this elegant square until 1908 when it was closed for failing to reach the required standards. It was opened in 1832 by John Preston, a Stokesley lawyer. What is now the annual Agriculture Show and Fair was established in 1223 when John Fitz-Robert de Eure was granted a charter by Henry III. It was founded in 1859 with a meeting held in The Golden Lion on the High Street (now Chapters Hotel). In addition there were cattle fairs, servant-hiring fairs twice a year and a cattle auction each Monday.

Church of St Peter and St Paul

Built in 1771 on the site of a pre-Norman conquest church, *Domesday* mentions a church here and a priest. Lady Anne Baliol, sister of the founder of the Oxford College, is buried in the church and Robert "Mouseman" Thompson's work can be found inside. Nearby is Stokesley Manor House, known as "The Castle" and now council offices. The gate piers are from Angrove Hall, demolished in 1832. In the eighteenth century Roman Catholics had a "mass house" close to the Manor House (which at the time was inhabited by a family of recusants); *The Gentleman's Magazine* for January 1746 tells us that it was attacked by a mob of Stokesley youths who broke in through the roof, ransacked it and burnt their spoils at the market cross, exclaiming *"God save King George and down with the mass!"*

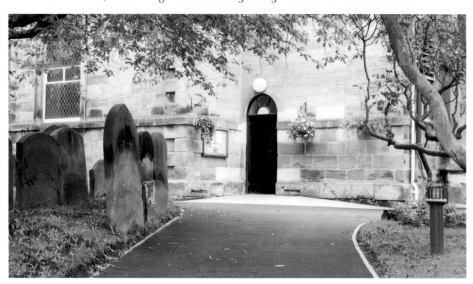

Packhorse Bridge

On Levenside, a fine example of a seventeenth-century packhorse bridge behind the Queen's Head pub taken in 1961, described as follows by T. Whellan in his *History of Stokesley* of 1859: *"an ancient bridge of one segmental arch , narrow and steep."*

Union Mill

Beyond the iron bridge further upstream was Union Mill, a linen mill active around the early nineteenth century to support Stokesley's brief flirtation with the linen industry; the mill built in 1823 had been demolished by 1850, and Candlemaker's Yard is also there. Armstrong Richardson, recently rebranded as Millbry Hill, has been trading nearby for over eighty years selling animal products and feed.

West Green and the Wizard of Stokesley

West Green showing some of the elegant houses for which Stokesley is well known, many going back to the seventeenth and eighteenth centuries. The first white woman to settle in Victoria, Australia in 1836, Jane Pace (born 1817), was from Stokesley; in 1934 trees were planted on South Levenside in her memory. But more famous is John Wrightson, wise man or witch doctor, who was sentenced to gaol at Northallerton for his alleged crimes. Unjustly says J. C. Atkinson (see page 39). The *Malton Messenger* of 5 September 1863 reports: *"He was taken away in a horse-drawn Black Maria and poisoned himself as it passed through Hovingham."* Wrightson habitually wore flowing robes and a wizard's pointed hat adorned with astrological signs; it seems that he was nothing more than a harmless quack administering to the minor ailments of men and animals.

Vandalism at Fidler's Mill
Probably the same mill that is
mentioned in *Domesday*, Fidler's
Mill was demolished in 1983,
despite local protests, along
with the adjacent mill cottage.
Notwithstanding this vandalism
the Stokesley Society managed to
salvage the mill wheel from the
rubble, restoring it to stand today at
the eastern approach to the village.

Danby Parish Church

Two miles outside Danby in Danby Dale, near to where the original Danish village was, consisting of wooden buildings, St Hilda's Church has a fifteenth-century tower and an eighteenth-century nave. It was restored in 1903. John Christopher Atkinson (1814-1900) is buried there – ornithologist and author of the famous *Forty Years in a Moorland Parish* which describes the 70,000 miles he is said to have covered walking the moors over fifty years. He was vicar for fifty-three years and died in 1900 but not before he had married three times and fathered thirteen children. Danby Castle built in the early 1300s is now a farm and used for the meetings of the Danby Court Leet and Baron established in 1656. It is reached by crossing the 1836 Duck Bridge and was once the seat of the Latimers; Catharine Parr lived there when she married John Latimer after the death of Henry VIII. The drawing of the church is from the cover of the *Danby Parish Magazine*, November 1933.

Castleton and the Hand of Glory

Castleton got its name from the triple-moated twelfth century Norman castle built by the de Brus family. The church is dedicated to St Michael and St George. The altar has wooden side panels bearing the signature mice of Robert Thompson. From the early 1800s a cheese fair has been held here, underlining the importance of cheese in the neighbourhood; at one point it is estimated that local farmers produced an average two tons per year. The "Hand of Glory" was found in Hawthorn Cottage in the High Street (now a bank). This was the hand of a criminal who died on the gibbet; it was drained of blood, cured in saltpetre and pepper and dried for two weeks; a candle was then placed in its clutch with a wick made from the hair of the corpse; it was then used by burglars to illuminate the houses they were burgling. The alleged magic properties of the hand ensured that the occupants remained asleep for the duration of the raid; if they did wake they would have been petrified at the sight of the glowing hand. The only way to break the spell was to drench the hand in blood or skimmed milk. Today the hand can be seen in the Pannett Museum at Whitby.

Lealholm Floods 1963

Golden Flake Tobacco and Capstan Cigarettes feature on the advertisements in the village shop window. Note the floodwater up to roof level at some of the outhouses. Lealholm boasts some of the most extensive rock gardens in England following the course of Crunkly Gill through the village. These are largely due to the efforts of Sir Francis Ley. John Castillo – poet, stonemason and preacher – was born here and died in 1845; a cottage called Poet's Cottage now stands on the site of his original house. The ancient Court Leet still administers the village's common land from Danby. The Glaisdale and Lealholme Society for the Prosecution of Felons still exists. Two Edwardian water taps complete with iron goblets on chains can still be seen today. Lealholm seems to have suffered very badly in the two world wars with the memorial showing forty-three fallen in the First World War and thirteen in the Second World War.

Making Besoms in Glaisdale

A fascinating picture of a dying country craft: George and Isaac Scarth making besoms at Rock Head Cottage. Sandstone from the sixteenth and eighteenth century quarries was used in the building of Waterloo Bridge. Iron ore was discovered here in the late eighteenth century leading to the construction of two chimneys, one 250 feet high, as well as three furnaces and a population explosion from 600 to 2,000. Houses and a Mechanics' Institute were built to accommodate and educate the miners. Glaisdale played an important role in the rise of Middlesbrough as a major steel town in the nineteenth and twentieth centuries. The modern picture was taken above Rock Head Farm.

Counting Sheep in Glaisdale

Willie Coates relaxing with his sheep dog amongst the sheep near Quarry Farm. His daughter Eliza is strolling on the path. Today, photographer Mark Sunderland reflects how nothing could be further removed from the grim, pessimistic picture painted by the journalist in a York newspaper in 1858 who wrote about *"the devastating effects of the iron mines and the new line of railway, which will entirely change the face of the scenery."*

Glaisdale Bridge Accident and Beggar's Bridge

A terrible accident on a bridge over the Esk at Glaisdale. The Esk is bridged three times at Glaisdale. The best known, Beggar's Bridge, was built by Thomas Ferries in 1619. To meet Agnes Richardson the squire's daughter and the love of his life, Thomas had to wade through the river. When he asked for Agnes' hand in marriage the squire refused because he was *"no more than a beggar"*. Understandably miffed at this Thomas went off to Whitby and joined the navy seeing action against the Spanish. As a pirate under Drake he won a share of a sizable booty from a captured galleon and returned to Glaisdale a wealthy man, eventually becoming Mayor of Hull and Warden of Trinity House in Hull in 1820. The squire now relented and Agnes and Thomas were married; Thomas pledged that no man should ever get his feet wet crossing the river and paid for Beggar's Bridge to be built.

The North York Moors Railway

NYMR Railway Letter Service stamps showing the Moorlander passing the signal box at Grosmont station. Grosmont was originally built to accommodate the railway workers and was originally called Tunnel; but the name had changed by 1394 to commemorate the 1204 Benedictine priory founded by Johanna Fossard and monks from Grandimont in Normandy. The Whitby to Pickering line here was endorsed by George Stephenson and opened in 1835 carrying 6,000 passengers in the first three months – including Charles Dickens. The complete line opened in 1836 with trees and heather wrapped in sheepskins being used as foundation for the tracks in boggy areas. The line also transported iron ore from the mines to Whitby (100,000 tons were mined annually at one point); the mine closed in 1871, the line closed in 1965. The North York Moors Railway Preservation Society was formed in 1967 with 9,000 members; they bought the section of the line from Grosmont to Eller Beck and the North York Moors Railway opened in 1973; 300,000 journeys are made each year. Tunnel survives as the northern terminus of the line.

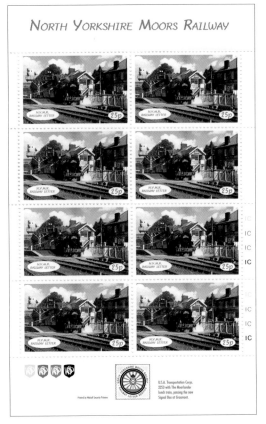

St Mary's Goathland

The 1896 St Mary's Church pictured here in 1909 has as one of its treasures a fine mid fifteenth-century gold and silver chalice. Another is the Saxon font brought from Egton when the church there was demolished in 1878. St Mary's predecessor was a twelfth-century thatched chapel serving the Hermitage of Godeland: Osmund the Priest and his brethren were charged to pray for the soul of Queen Matilda and to *"lodge and entertain the poor."*

The Mallyan Spout Hotel
Named after the waterfall – the tallest in the North York Moors at 70 feet, the hotel dates back to 1892. Goathland was of course the setting for the village of Aidensfield in the popular soap, *Heartbeat*. The name Aidensfield was arrived at after a visit to St Mary's church and members of the crew saw stained glass pictures of St Aidan.

Goathland Village and Moors

FRITH
74322

The Plough Stots Sword Dance

A Viking fertility dance survives here in the form of the Plough Stots Sword Dance performed annually on the first Saturday after Plow Monday. The dance is intended to banish evil spirits and guarantee a good harvest and latterly took the form of locals dragging their ploughs around the village collecting beer money – refusal to contribute apparently led to your garden being ploughed up. The headquarters of the Goathland Plough Stots dance team is in the Goathland Hotel where you can still see the "swords" over the fireplace arranged in the Star of Bethlehem formation of the dance.

The Common, Goathland

FRITH GHD.B

Goathland

The beginning and the end of the 54 mile Crosses Walk taking in 13 moorland crosses. In 1117 St Mary's Hermitage was established at Godeland; St Mary's name lives on in the present church. The village pound used to pen stray animals was in use here until 1924.

Hogsmeade Station

Built in 1865 this quaint halt is probably most famous now as Hogsmeade Station, the stop for Hogwarts School of Witchcraft and Wizardry in *Harry Potter and the Philosopher's Stone;* the Hogwarts Express stops here on arrival from platform 9¾ at King's Cross. According to J. K. Rowling's instructions, Hogsmeade station is not in Hogsmeade, but on the opposite side of the lake. The final scene in the film has the train leaving Hogsmeade station, and thanks to special effects, with Hogwarts castle in the background. The dramatic painting of Goathland station is by John Freeman.

Beck Hole 1939 and the Game of Quoits

Algernon Newton RA painted the sign on the Birch Hall Inn to the right here – one of the few inn signs to be painted by a member of the Royal Academy. A notice in the pub describes the ancient game of quoits which is still played on the village green in a local league. Each quoit is 5½ pounds in weight and the hub to be reached is 11 yards away, so the advice on the notice is quite apt: "the throwing of the quoit is a test of skill, judgement and strength." Beck Hole is part of the Duchy of Lancaster; some of the cottages around the green date back to 1728.

Carlton's Revd George Sangar and a Case of Arson?

Pony and trap, Edwardian girls and the Blackwell Ox pub on the left in this 1904 shot. The dilapidated church here, St Botolph's, was reputedly rebuilt by one of the vicars, the Revd George Sangar who raised the money and worked on it day and night himself. Completed in 1879 it was destroyed by fire two years later. Sangar was charged with arson but acquitted. The present St Botolph's is somewhat quirky with the tower half in and half out the nave. Carlton has two fine houses: the mid 1700s Busby Hall, home of the Marwoods, which the ironmaster John Gjers rented in the early twentieth century; and the Queen Anne style Manor House, built by Captain Christopher Prissick, the owner of the alum works on Carlton Bank, in 1707. The Blackwell Ox pub is named after a shorthorn bull bred near Darlington.

Carlton Belles

3 June 1908 saw the celebrations in Carlton to raise the £800 needed for the new eight bell peal at St Botolph's church; it attracted people from miles around, was organised by Canon Kyle and led by the Carlton Belles. Each bell carries a special inscription; they include Annie Gjers, Strangers', Village and Children's. The modern picture shows metalwork outside G. Ward & Sons – General and Wrought Ironsmith opposite the Methodist church.

Canon Kyle in the Fox and Hounds

The pony and trap have moved on a bit. Temple Moor designed the new fourteenth-century church under Kyle's close guidance. It was completed in three years at the modest cost of £2,696. Local stone and labour was used and there were no stained glass windows so as to allow the trees outside to be seen from the inside. The lych gate is another Kyle-inspired feature. Canon John Latimer Kyle had been vicar here for forty-nine years by the time of his death in 1943. He bought the Fox and Hounds pub next door to the vicarage managing it with the same enthusiasm and vigour as he did his ministry. To fend off the inevitable criticism he met from church colleagues he agreed to impose a six-day license whereby the inn remained closed on Sundays. He is also responsible for setting up one of the first youth clubs in the country – over the stables at the inn. The pub closed in 1969 and is now a private house.

Church of the Holy Cross, Swainby

This 1877 church replaces the original Norman church of the same name which was at Whorlton. A school was opened in this delightful village in 1728 (now a hairdresser's). The school in Church Street replaced this in 1856 (The Whorlton Parochial School) funded by public subscription and in 1968 was in turn replaced by the one that exists today in Claver Close. A Wesleyan Chapel opened in 1850 and a Primitive Chapel in 1851, both now closed. William Clowes held a Primitive Methodist open-air meeting on Scarth Nick in 1820 – allegedly attended by over 2000 people. An Oddfellows Hall was built in 1863 which in 1921 became the Village Hall.

Swainby and the River Leven

Swainby is named after the swains who worked on the estate farms of West Laithes and West Leeths and who lived here. Roman coins found in the river suggest Roman activity of some sort. Swainby first appears in records in 1368 and its settlement may be due to the Black Death driving the ten surviving inhabitants down the hill from Whorlton in 1428. Ironstone and jet mining in the mid 1800s led to some local prosperity and a surge in population. Some of these cottages go back as far as 1718.

The Miner's Arms and Henry Cooper

One of three pubs up until recently in Swainby, the others were and still are the Blacksmith's Arms and the Black Horse. The picture shows licensees Len and Lillian Willison outside the Miner's Arms; it closed in 2008 and is now a private house. Donkeys used by miners here grazed on Live Moor. Nearby Scugdale was the birthplace of Elizabeth Harland who died in 1812 age 105 and of Henry Cooper a giant who grew to 8ft 6ins. The contemporary *1890 North Riding Directory* tells us *"this remarkable sample of humanity grew 13 inches in the space of 5 months."* He went to London and joined Barnum & Bailey's circus touring the USA with them. He returned to England sporting the name Sir Henry Alexander Cooper but died aged thirty-two.

Whorlton Church. 100

Whorlton Old Church

The fifteenth-century tower remains as does a stone cross and an oak effigy of a man and a dog in a canopied tomb from around 1400. The last service there took place on 7 March 1875. Sir James Strangeways' Whorlton Estate passed to Matthew, Earl of Lennox on his death in 1541; Lennox's wife was a niece of Henry VIII. The Estate was given to Thomas Bruce in 1604 by their son, James I, and remained in the family until 1887 when James Emerson of Easby Manor bought it. The Bruces chopped the woods down and divided Whorlton Great Park into five farms.

Whorlton Castle

An early nineteenth-century lithograph showing the gatehouse and what's left of the rest of the castle. The motte and bailey in the original wooden castle was built by Robert de Meynell on the site of a Brigantian fortification and a later Roman fort. By 1343 it was *"ruinous"* and rebuilt in stone later in the century by John Darcy. By the late 1500s it was dilapidated again. *Domesday* tells us that Whorlton was a place of some importance; it was originally Whorl Hill or Worm Hill named after the giant worm that lived there terrorising the locals until a baron from the castle slew it. The plot to marry Mary Queen of Scots to Lord Darnley was hatched here. A hoard of fourth-century silver Roman coins and other artefacts was discovered here in 1810. In 1956 Len Willison rented Whorlton Castle for £2.00 per year and used it to keep free range chickens.

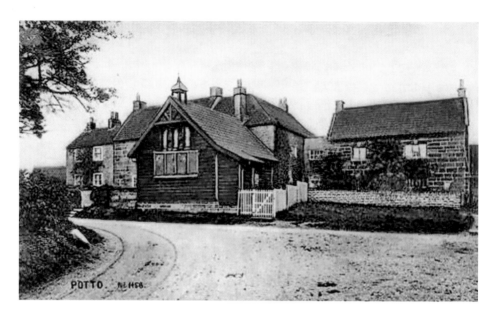

Preston's of Potto and the Lyke Wake Walk

The village of Potto is famous for three things. Anyone who has ever driven on Britain's roads and motorways will be familiar with the ubiquitous haulage vehicles of Preston's of Potto based here. The company was established in 1936 by Richard Preston and originally operated as an agricultural business; the transport division was formed in 1957. Secondly, the Lyke Wake Walk: named after the Cleveland Lyke Wake Dirge sang over the coffins of those to be transported the 42 miles over the moors to Ravenscar (lyke means corpse, wake, watch). It was believed that the soul had to cross the moors to reach Paradise. Bill Cowley lived in Potto and established the walk, making the first crossing in October 1955. In the late 1950s Potto became notorious as the village with "the pub that never opened". If you wanted to go in, the owner, a Mr Heslop, would peer through the window to see if he liked the look of you or not before allowing entry.

Osmotherley

Originally Osmunderly from the Old Norse meaning Osmund's Ley and Asmundrelac – Asmund's clearing. The 5-pillared stone barter table here was originally a market stall and used by John Wesley as a pulpit; he visited the village no less than sixteen times. One of the first Methodist chapels in England was built here in 1754. Other places of worship abound: an early sixteenth-century Lady Chapel restored in 1960 as a place of pilgrimage and the old hall, a Quaker Meeting House and St Peter's Parish Church. Mount Grace Priory – Britain's best-preserved Carthusian monastery – is nearby.

Osmotherley Cross

An alternative derivation of the name comes from the legend whereby a soothsayer fortold the death by drowning of King Oswald's son, Oswy. To prevent this his distraught mother took him up Roseberry Topping but she fell asleep and Oswy fell into a pool watered by a spring and drowned. She buried him at a place called Teviotdale which took the name *Os-by his-mother-lay* when she died and was buried next to him. Osmotherley had a linen industry in the eighteenth, nineteenth and early twentieth centuries producing sailcloth and later coverings for aeroplane wings. The youth hostel was a flax mill in the 1800s.

Chequer's Inn and the Fire that Won't Go Out

800 feet above sea level the turf fire in the Chequer's – a 300-year-old drover's inn – is reputed to have been burning constantly for 200 years. The sign says *"Be not in haste, step in and taste – Ale tomorrow for nothing."* It disappeared in 1965 later turning up in Northallerton and eventually replaced in 1984. Chequer's was patronised by smugglers, one of whom is said to be buried under the fire. Osmotherley was also noted and for the alum, jet, coal and ironstone mines nearby.

Chop Gate

Chop Gate from the Norse *kaup* and pronounced locally as Chop Yat can be roughly translated as Pedlar Street after the chapmen who called on the farms and cottages selling various household items. As the pictures show, little has changed over the years in this typical Moors village.

Saltersgate – Hole of Horcum

Saltersgate is the old salt road from the coast to York – much frequented by smugglers. Saltersgate Inn at the bottom of the hill was once a coaching inn with a tollbooth and, like the Chequers Inn (see page 63) has a peat fire which has been burning for over 200 years (since 1801 in this case). The Hole is a massive hollow said to have been created by a giant or by the devil. The giant Wade scooped up the earth to throw at Bell, his wife. Or, the devil gouged it out and threw it over the moors and thus formed Blakey Topping. Sadly, Mother Nature explains it all away as the endless work of the many springs there.

Fylingdales and the Three Minute Warning

The seventh-century Lilla Cross is on the moor here – one of the oldest Christian monuments in northern England. Lilla was a servant of King Edwin of Deira; he was killed in 626 when trying to protect his master from a poisoned dagger attack. Edwin later converted to Christianity and built a church on the site of York Minster. The twentieth-century Ballistic Missile Early Warning Station pictured here was built in 1962; Pevsner described it as *"the geometry of the space age at its most alluring and frightening."* Each radome weighed 100 tons, was 154ft high and 140ft in diameter; they were made of 1646 laminated glass fibre panels (hexagonal and pentagons). The 84ft diameter radars inside swivelled around and had a range of 300 miles. It cost £54 million and was only ever out of commission once for twelve hours; 900 people were employed there in the 1960s; nowadays it's nearer 400. The three radomes have now been replaced by the pyramid-shaped Solid State Phased Array Radars (SSPARs); each comprises 2,560 transmit/receive modules; total peak power output is about 2.5MW, with a tracking range of over 3,000 miles. Wow!

Rosedale Abbey

Named loosely after the Benedictine nine nun and a prioress priory founded here by Robert de Stuteville in 1158. This late eighteenth-century sketch shows the ruins before most of them were quarried to provide housing for the Victorian mineworkers. All that now remains is a small turret or belfry with a stone spiral staircase; they can be found close to the 1839 church of St Mary and St Laurence. Thriving on sales of wool for many years (in a good year they sold twelve sacks) the priory closed after the Dissolution in 1538. The first industry here, though, was illegal glassmaking established by Huguenots in the early sixteenth century. One of their furnaces (25 feet long, 18 feet wide and 3½ feet high) is now in the Ryedale Folk Museum in Hutton-le-Hole (see page 73).

GEAR AT EAST SIDE MINES

ENTRANCE . E. MINES

RUINED KILNS E. SIDE

**ROSEDALE
MINES
IRONSTONE
WORKING
1856 – 1926**

SHERRIFF'S PIT

EAST SIDE MINES

Rosedale Mines

Mines were sunk hereabouts to extract the ore which was calcined (burnt) in kilns to reduce its weight (coal being brought in from the Durham coalfields for this). The wagon and horse transportation to Pickering was replaced in 1861 by a fourteen-mile railway from Battersby to Bank Top here. The height of the 100 feet chimney built here for the mine had been specified by a landowner anxious that the grouse on his land were not upset by it and gives its name to the steep 1:3 road up from Rosedale–Chimney Bank. Sadly, it was demolished in 1972 because the £6,000 needed to restore it could not be raised. Mining had begun in 1851 and between 1856 and 1885 three million tons of iron ore were mined; the population around about grew from 500 to 3,000 but the "Klondyke" was over by 1922 and the mine was closed in 1926 after the General Strike. The card shows (l-r) loading gear at east side mines; entrance to east side mines; ruined kilns at east side mines, east side mines and Sherrif's Pit.

Rosedale Mines Railways

The fourteen-mile Rosedale Bank extension to the Ingleby-Kildale line was opened on 27 March 1861. The one mile incline climbed to 1,370 feet at gradients between 1:9 and 1:5 and the wagons were hauled with steel ropes 1,650 feet long around 14 feet drums taking three minutes at 20 mph per journey. Some of the railway workers lived in the cottages at Little Blakey. The construction of the incline was not without incident: *The Malton Messenger* reports: a riot by 60 navvies ransacked *"the pub of Mr Sturdy helping themselves to liquor and victuals, some carried heavy bludgeons...[they] set on Mr Towns, who was knocked on to the floor bleeding and shouting 'murder.'"* At its peak the railway carried a daily average of 1,000 tons of iron ore.

TRAIN AT THE DEPOTS ROSEDALE EAST TERMINUS

TRAIN AT SLEDSHOE BANK TOP TERMINUS

SLOWATH LEVEL CROSSING CABLE INCLINE ABOVE INGLEBY

PLOUGHING SNOW 1300# UP BLAKEY JUNCTION. AD 1900.

ROSEDALE MINERAL RAILWAY
1860 - 1929

Hawnby and the Sultan of Zanzibar

The seventeenth-century Arden Hall, seat of the Earls of Mexborough is here. Mary Queen of Scots spent a night here just before her execution. John Wesley said of his visit there: "I rode through one of the pleasantest parts of England to Hawnby." Nearby lived George Baxter, better known as the Hermit of Rosedale or, as he liked to call himself, *Lord Rosedale, Sultan of Zanzibar, Admiral of the French Fleet*. George lived in virtual isolation resolutely refusing to pay his bills – attempts to persuade him were often met by a salvo from his double-barrelled shotgun. Even an aptly named PC Tom Shooter failed in his attempt to bring him to book. George died in 1959 and is buried in grave 1926 in Pickering churchyard. All Saints Church here features a poetry shrine.

Hutton-le-Hole Beer Houses and Quakers

Originally called Hotun (as in *Domesday*); then Hege-Hoton, Hotun under Heg, and Hewton in 1579. *Hutton* signifies the place near the burial mounds; *Hole* denotes the fact that Hutton lies in a hollow between two nabs. The Hammer & Hand beerhouse was built in 1784 by Emmanuel and Betty Strickland and bears the inscription *"By Hammer and Hand all Arts do Stand"*. It was next door to a blacksmith's which later became the Crown Inn. The well-named Boxing Tom (Tom Proud) was landlord in 1870. John Richardson lived in one of the cottages – a Quaker and good friend of Robert Penn's – he travelled far and wide in America working with native Indians as well as white men. There was a meeting house here and a Quaker burial ground nearby. Little has changed in this picturesque village in the fifty or so years between photographs.

Sutton Bank and Lake Gormire

Sutton-under-Whitestone-Cliff (one of the longest place names in Yorkshire) is the village at the foot of the bank whose 1:4 incline still continues to cause problems for winter traffic today. It is said that in the early days of motoring some drivers had to reverse up the bank. It takes the road from 120m metres above sea level to 300 metres in one mile. The reputedly bottomless 10,000-year-old Lake Gormire is below, complete with the massive boulders on its bed which fell from the cliff above in 1755 – a catastrophic event witnessed and described graphically by John Wesley who attributed it to the power of the Almighty. Some say that a complete village lies at the bottom of the lake, submerged due to the meanness of the inhabitants' when they each (bar one) refused an angel, dressed as a beggar, a cup of water. It is one of only three natural lakes in Yorkshire (the others being Malham Tarn and Semerwater) notable for the fact that no streams flow into it. Above is where the Yorkshire Gliding Club operates: their altitude record is 30,200 feet. The new photograph shows a glider taking off and the spectacular view the pilot gets when he or she goes over the edge...

Kilburn: the Horse and the Mouseman

Kilburn is at the southern end of the White Rose Walk, the other being at Roseberry Topping. It appears as Chilburne in *Domesday* and means a cell by a stream. Today it is world famous for two things: the White Horse and the work of Robert Thompson. Robert Thompson's Craftsmen's Ltd was set up by Robert Thompson; he was born in the Old Hall in 1872 and was inspired by fifteenth-century carvings in Ripon Cathedral to emulate medieval craftsmen. He died in 1955 age seventy-nine; the business is carried on today by his great grandsons Ian, Peter and Giles Cartwright and over thirty other workers; the Visitor Centre opened in 1994 and was refurbished in 2002. This 1920s picture shows timber being unloaded at the workshop – a scene still regularly repeated today.

Robert Thompson and Ampleforth

Pony and trap with the White Horse in the background of this 1903 shot of the village. Robert Thompson's work can be seen all over Yorkshire and indeed Britain. His favourite it seems was in the library of Ampleforth College where he worked from the 1920s to the 1950s when he retired. One of his earlier commissions was the wooden cross which stands in the graveyard at Ampleforth Abbey. This came about after a meeting with Father Paul Nevill, a monk at the abbey and parish priest in Ampleforth village, which also resulted in a refectory table and a chair for Ampleforth College, both still in use today. A refectory table today will set you back £8,110.

Mouseman's Cottage

This sixteenth-century building was Robert Thompson's home and design studio. Thompson's wood of choice was the oak; he used an adze in preference to a plane – a tool which created a wavy surface and emphasised the grain to beautiful effect – characteristics of Thompson's work – and his chosen style was classic seventeenth-century English. The famous mouse signature came about apparently when he heard one of his carvers, Charlie Barker, say "*We are all as poor as church mice*" whereupon Robert spontaneously carved a mouse on the church screen he was working on and took it up as a symbol of industry in quiet places, and as his trademark. The older photograph shows Robert Thompson in his workshop in 1897.

The Mouse Man Chapel

The Chapel of St Thomas in St Mary's Church was refitted as a shrine to Thompson soon after his death in 1958. The lectern in the church bears a carved crocodile as well as the famous mouse which also makes an appearance on the pulpit and on the desk in the sanctuary. The old schoolhouse in the village has a dedication from the villagers to Edward archbishop of York for his rebuilding and continued support of the school from 1841. The earlier picture shows craftsmen at work in the 1920s.

Three Horses and The White Horse 1909

With an eye big enough to seat twenty people the famous horse on Roulston Scar is 304 feet long and 228 feet high taking in two acres. 'Delivered' in 1857 by John Hodgson, the village schoolmaster and sometime surveyor with the help of thirty-three men, the lime needed to paint it weighed six tons. Although the largest of the eleven surviving White Horses in Britain, it is of course an imitation of the White Horse of Uffington in Berkshire. Thomas Taylor, a native of Kilburn and rich from his Yorkshire hams business in London, saw the Uffington horse and determined that Kilburn should have one of its own. It can be seen up to 40 miles away and was covered over in the Second World War so as not to provide a landmark for German planes.

Helmsley. Yorks.

Castlegate, Helmsley

The older Edwardian photograph shows the porch on the Old Manor House in Castlegate on the left with All Saints Church in the background. The name Helmsley derives from the Saxon for Helm's Clearing *(Ulmetum* in the *Anglo Saxon Chronicle)*; then Hamelake and to the Normans it was Elmeslac after the elms that stood there. *Domesday* tells us that it had three thegns, thirteen families, a wooden church, two priests and 11½ curucates of arable land (a curucate = the amount of land ploughable by an eight oxen team in one year, roughly 170 acres). The Lord of the Manor was Ughtred. William I gave Helmsley land to Robert de Moutain, his half brother, but when he rebelled against William Rufus in 1088 it passed to Walter l'Espec whom Abbot Aelred from Rievaulx described as *"having a voice like the sound of a trumpet".*

MARKET CROSS AND CHURCH, HELMSLEY L 1915

The Market Cross

The Market Cross with the buildings which were to be annexed to the Black Swan immediately behind and on the right and W. H. Atkinson's grocer's in the centre – now the NatWest bank. In 1887 Sarah J. Warriner's wholesale wine and spirit merchant, brewer and maltster in Market Place offered the following: *scotch whiskey 21s (£1.05p) per gallon; best Nicholson's gin 13s; bottle of claret 2s 6d; orange quinine wine 2s; gingerette 2s; Helmsley ale 1s 8d per gallon. Terms: no discount allowed after six month's credit.* On l'Espec's death Helmsley passed to Peter de Roos and then to his son, Robert whose surname was Furstan, one of the Guardians of the Magna Carta. In 1377 the plague wiped out most of Helmsley's adult population of 282. The population in 1801 was 1,449; in 1881 it was 2,377. The modern picture shows the market to be still in action – and Ryedale District Council's eye for the truly scenic.

Canon's Garth

The unofficial vicarage, this E-shaped timbered house in the churchyard is part twelfth century and part Tudor; the earlier part was built by Walter l'Espec to house the Augustinian canons of Kirkham Abbey. It was then owned by a John Manners, brother of the Earl of Rufford. It was split into two cottages in 1860, fell into disrepair and was restored in 1893 when it housed the Sisters of the Holy Rood. Around 1860 the illegitimacy rate in Helmsley was 15%; Canon Gray (see page 86) was warned not to raise the issue with unmarried mothers and the mother of one threatened to douse him in boiling water if he did.

The Roundhouse

The old police station was preceded by a domed building near the cross called the Roundhouse. In 1844 a man charged with skinning sheep committed suicide there and it was later closed down and a new police station built in 1857 to replace it. It was later used as a weighing room by the town's butchers. You can see the domed lock-up in this rare view of the square from around the 1840s. Today it is a café. Drawing courtesy of Helmsley Archaeological and Historical Society taken from their *A History of Helmsley, Rievaulx and District*.

Helmsley High Street

Looking down towards All Saints with the Feversham Arms on the far left. George Villiers, first Duke of Buckingham, inherited the estates here in 1632. Described as a *"chemist, fiddler, statesman and buffoon"* Villiers retired to Helmsley, repaired the castle and squandered the £50,000 per annum he earned in rents; he became a social outcast but not before he built a racecourse here to satisfy his love for all things equestrian. Sir Charles Duncombe, a wealthy London banker, bought the Helmsley estate in 1689 for £90,000 and engaged John Vanbrugh to build the Doric Duncombe House in 600 acres of land in 1718; this was achieved with the labour of 800 unemployed local men. The Duncombes became Earls of Feversham. The house was made into St Mary's Girls' School in the 1920s in an effort to pay the punitive death duties after the second earl was killed in action in 1916. It remained a school until 1985 and was opened to the public in 1990.

HELMSLEY MARKET PLACE No 335.

The Feversham Monument

A busy 1916 market day in the Market Place. Designed by Sir Gilbert Scott the statue sculpted by Mathew Noble has Feversham in his peer's robes. The dedication reads: *"To William Second Baron of Feversham. This monument is erected by his tenantry, friends and relatives who cherish his memory with affection and gratitude. Born 1798, died 1867."* King Edward VII (as Duke of York) came to Helmsley in 1901 to lay the foundation stone of the new Town Hall on the left here designed by Temple Moor; it served as courthouse and market hall and replaced the old tollbooth. Before the Town Hall was built in 1901 the site was occupied by York & East Riding Bank. To the right of the Town Hall is the old police station; a new police station was built in 1857, now a café; next door is the Golden Lion. The railways came to Helmsley in 1871 when the line to Gilling was opened; Kirbymoorside followed in 1874 and Pickering the following year. In 1823 postmaster Thomas Pape in Castlegate received letters from York at 5 am and sent post back at 2 pm; since 1680 this was carried by boys on horses required to travel at 7 mph in summer and 5 mph in winter.

BLACK SWAN HOTEL, HELMSLEY   N9336.

The Black Swan and the Wordsworths

William and Dorothy Wordsworth stayed here in 1802 on the way to visit William's future wife, Mary Hutchinson at Gallows Hill Brompton-by-Sawdon, near Scarborough. Dorothy tells us in her diaries that they *"slept at a very nice inn and were well treated."* All three stayed there again (or was it the Golden Lion, now a butcher's?) on the journey back from the wedding. On this occasion Dorothy's diaries tell us, *"My heart danced at the sight of its cleanly outside, bright yellow walls, casements overshadowed with jasmine, and low, double gabled-ended front."* During the Civil War while the castle was being besieged the house was ransacked by Cromwell's soldiers: *"defased, outhouses pulled down, and furnetaur taken away."* Five other inns existed in 1823: The Board (now the Feversham Arms), The Crown, The New Inn (a posting-house in Borogate), The Golden Lion and the Royal Oak in Market Place. A coach, *The Helmsley Highflyer*, ran from The Black Swan between Richmond and York in 1838 leaving for York at 9 am on Mondays, Wednesday and Fridays. As well as the pub sign itself there is a sign for Robinson's livery stables to the right in this Edwardian picture.

A hunting we will go!

And hungry, homeward
will return

To feast away the night.

For a hunting we will go!

*What about "Tiny's"
promised card?
Thanks for your
kind invitation
to "Supper" for march
25 th / 05.*

1901   ROTARY PHOTO. E.C.

A Meet Outside The Black Swan

A 1905 shot of a meet outside The
Black Swan – always popular with
country sportsmen and women.
Apart from the usual fox hunting
meets the pub is still the focal point
for shooting parties, particularly
pheasant shooting; a gunroom and
drying room caters for their needs.
Earliest references are in 1784. It
now comprises three buildings: the
Georgian in the middle, known as
Bankins House and the home of the
Sandwith family from 1725, annexed
in 1947; the fifteenth century half-
timbered Old Rectory on the left
added in 1949 and the Elizabethan
building on the right – the site of
the original inn and featuring a
fifteenth-century doorway quarried
from the castle. This also revealed
its wattle and daub walls during the
conversion. The pub has no name on
the sign, the wooden swan speaks for
itself, recently turned round to hide
the weathering the other side has
endured.

Bondgate

Bondgate was the first street to be tarred in 1911 and has some of the town's oldest buildings, notably the old bakehouse which was an example of the cruck method. This shows The Black Swan and The Crown next door; you can see the crown sign on the inn at the middle window on the left. The Wesleyan chapel was built here in 1800 and enlarged in 1852 at the same time as a Wesleyan Day School was built. The Roman Catholic church was built on the road to Rievaulx. One of the more celebrated and colourful vicars of All Saint's from 1870 to his death in 1913 was the staunchly anti-Catholic and anti-Methodist Revd Charles Norris Gray (son of Robert, Metropolitan Bishop of Capetown). Amongst his pet grievances he managed to put right were the lack of good sanitation – the town drain contained *"enough filth to poison everyone"*, housing – *"utterly unfit for man or beast...no house need be dirty...a woman is worth nothing if she cannot keep her house clean"* – over-long hours for apprentices, publication of one of the first parish magazines, the over-tight lacing of stays and the abolition of uniforms for children in the poor house so as to make them inconspicuous in the town.

Helmsley from Bridge

Helmsley from the Bridge

Very little has changed in this view of Helmsley. In 1754 Boro Beck flooded: thirteen people drowned and thirteen buildings were destroyed and most of Rye Bridge was swept away. Duncombe Park can boast England's first Ha-Ha, England's tallest ash tree (148 feet) and England's tallest lime tree (154 feet). The Nelson Gate on the York road bears the following inscription: *"To the memory of Lord Viscount Nelson, and the unparalleled gallant achievements of the British Navy; Lamented Hero! O! Price his conquering country grieved to pay! O dear bought glories of Trafalgar's day."*

All Saints and Vicar Gray's Frescoes

Part of the tower is thirteenth-century, the south doorway is Norman with a eleventh century hogback. You can also see the three lances which used to be carried into the market place by constables, the wooden yoke taken from a slave by the Metropolitan Bishop of Cape Town (father of Charles Norris Gray and friend of David Livingstone) and one of Livingstone's letters written from Africa. The pseudo-medieval frescoes in the south transept were designed by Vicar Gray in 1909 and depict the lives of St Aidan and St Oswald, St Columba founding Iona and a knight driving a huge six-metre dragon over a cliff edge (or the Saint of God driving Satan from Anglia). Gray's other major achievements include the restoration of the near derelict St William's College in York; the establishment of the open air service at Rievaulx and the historical pageant at the castle which in its second year attracted 5,000 people in 1898 from as far afield as Hartlepool, Hull and Leeds. Amazingly 170 children were taught to sing the *de Profundis* and the *Magnificat* in Latin for the occasion.

Helmsley Castle Barbican from the South

The castle dates from 1186 and is notable for its double defensive system of banks and ditches; it was built by Walter l'Espec (*d.* 1154 and one of the English leaders in the 1138 Battle of the Standard against the Scots), founder of the nearby Kirkham and Rievaulx abbeys. The castle was slighted after the Civil War by Cromwell after Sir Jordan Crossland tried to hold out against Thomas Fairfax in a 3-month siege when a relief force from Knaresborough and Skipton failed in its objective. The defenders were allowed to go free *"without aine molestacon".* Other notable surviving features include the thirteenth-century barbican pierced with loopholes for longbow men. Fairfax, according to Thomas Gill, in his *Vallis Eboracensis "received a musket-ball in his shoulder, and was carried off all but dead to York where for some time he vibrated between life and death."*

Fursan Castle

Sometimes called Fursan Castle, some parts predate l'Espec's castle and were built by Robert de Roos, Lord of Helmsley 1186-1227. This is one of two gates: one in the northwest wall the other in the south east and strengthened with a barbican. The keep is to the left, domestic buildings in the centre and the west tower to the right. A *garderobe* or latrine tower was built into the gateway's east tower: in effect this was a hole down the castle wall leading to the moat into which excrement was tipped. Clothes were hung at the top of the hole as it was believed that the powerful stench emanating from the fetid mess below deterred moths – hence garderobe – looking after your clothes.

Helmsley Hall

Midway along the western wall is the old hall, converted into a manor house between 1563 and 1587 by Edward Manners. This room, probably a parlour, was 39½ feet by 19½ feet and lit by four windows. The Tudor fireplace you can see here features an inlaid oak overmantel in Jacobean style. The old picture shows a charming domestic scene complete with pet bird and dog. As the modern photograph shows, little has changed.

CXD.J THE VILLAGE, COXWOLD

Copyright
Frith's

The Fauconberg Arms

The pub here on the right, the Fauconberg Arms, is named after the Fauconberg Hospital, a 1662 almhouse for *"ten poor and infirm men"*, now old people's homes. The pub bears the somewhat self-deprecating motto: *"Bonne et Belle Assez"*. Nearby Colville Hall was the old Manor House and the 1603 Old Hall was a free grammar school, now a private house.

St Michael's Church and a Headless Oliver Cromwell

Laurence Sterne was parson at the fifteenth-century St Michael's Church which stands on the site of a Norman predecessor. Among its treasures are its octagonal tower, a sixteenth-century Spanish sword forged in Toledo, a copy of the Geneva Bible printed in 1601 (the Breeches Bible) in a case made by Robert Thompson, coloured bosses and fifteenth-century glass. Mary Cromwell, Oliver's daughter, who married Thomas Ballasis, first Earl of Fauconberg, is buried here. Oliver himself (minus his head) was reputedly entombed by Mary in a bricked up attic room in Newburgh Priory, founded in 1145 as an Augustinian Friary, nearby. A silver screw-top pen bearing his initials is there; whether he is is another matter. The modern shot shows the wildflower area in front of the church.

Shandy Hall, Laurence Sterne and the Body Snatchers

Originally a medieval priest's house this was the home of Lawrence Sterne (*b.* 1713) for the last eight years of his life. He wrote *A Sentimental Journey Through France and Italy* and *Sermons of Mr Yorick* here as well as seven of the nine volumes of *The Life and Opinions of Tristram Shandy*. Sterne died of pleurisy in London in 1768; he was buried in the churchyard here but only after a circuitous journey. He was originally interred in St George's churchyard, Hanover Square, London, but his body was snatched by 'resurrection men' for use in medical dissection at Cambridge University. The cadaver was recognised by the Professor of Anatomy who fainted when he saw it on the table; it was hastily reburied. In 1969 the Lawrence Sterne Society obtained permission to remove his remains to Coxwold for re-burial here.

Tristram Shandy

Published over ten years from 1759-1769 *The Life and Opinions of Tristram Shandy, Gentleman* soon came to be regarded to be as one of the great comic novels in English. This LNER poster from the 1930s by Austin Cooper shows characters from the novel outside Shandy Hall. The modern picture shows the 2010 graphic version of the book by Martin Rowson.

Dr Slop

Shandy Hall is now a museum housing, among other things, the world's largest collection of Sterne's manuscripts and first editions. The Hogarth sketch shows Dr Slop snoozing in the parlour at Shandy Hall as Corporal Trim reads the Sermon. The new picture shows Sterne's library as it is today. Dr Slop was based on a Dr John Burton who lived in the Red House in York, now an antiques centre. Burton was a gynaecologist and writer; his books included *An Essay Towards a Complete System of Midwifery*, illustrated by no less an artist than George Stubbs who had come to York to learn his anatomy. He ended up teaching medical students before moving on to perfecting his comparative anatomy and painting his famous horse paintings.